Read All About Whales

# BALEEN WHALES

**Jason Cooper**

**The Rourke Corporation, Inc.**
**Vero Beach, Florida 32964**

PHOTO CREDITS
©Brandon Cole: cover, p.7, 16; ©Lynn M. Stone: p.6, 22; © Frank S. Balthis: p.9; ©Mark Conlin/INNERSPACE VISIONS: p.12, 18; ©Marty Snyderman: p.15, 20; ©Peter C. Howorth: p.4, 13, 19; ©Michael Nolan/INNERSPACE VISIONS: p.10


**Library of Congress Cataloging-in-Publication Data**

Cooper, Jason, 1942-
   Baleen whales / by Jason Cooper
      p. cm. — (Read all about whales)
   Includes index.
   Summary: Describes several different kinds of baleen whales, which have jaws lined with plates of baleen instead of teeth.
   ISBN 0-86593-450-9
   1. Baleen whales—Juvenile literature. [1. Baleen whales. 2. Whales.]
I. Title II. Series: Cooper, Jason, 1942-  Read all about whales
QL737.C42C66 1996
599.5'1—dc20                                              96–19191
                                                              CIP
                                                              AC


**Printed in the USA**

# TABLE OF CONTENTS

# BALEEN WHALES

You don't have to have big teeth to be a big eater! Most of the world's largest whales are toothless. Instead of having teeth, their upper jaws are lined with rows of **baleen** (buh LEEN), or whalebone.

The biggest of the baleen whales is the blue. It's probably the largest animal of all time.

Blues and other baleen whales used to be hunted, mostly for their meat, baleen, and oil. The killing left many baleen whales **endangered** (en DAYN jerd)—in danger of disappearing.

*A blue whale with jaws wide open strains food through its baleen.*

# BALEEN

Baleen, called whalebone, isn't bone at all. It's made of **keratin** (KER uh tin), the same substance that's in human fingernails.

Baleen plates hang from the top of a whale's mouth. The inside edge of each plate has brushlike bristles.

*The skeleton of a minke whale at the Pratt Museum of Natural History in Homer, Alaska, shows its baleen "brushes."*

*A humpback whale's throat bulges as it snacks on herring that its baleen filter from the sea.*

Each **species** (SPEE sheez), or kind, of baleen whale has a different number of plates. Some whales have as many as 400 on each side of their mouths.

The shape of the baleen plates differs from one species to another.

# WHALE FOOD

Most of the baleen whales are truly giant **mammals** (MAM uhlz). The blue whale reaches 100 feet in length!

Despite their size, baleen whales live on tiny **plankton** (PLANK ton) and small fish. Plankton are the little creatures, such as shrimplike krill, that drift through the sea.

The whale's baleen traps plankton from tons of seawater that it swishes through its mouth.

*Baleen whales strain tons of seawater for small fish and tiny plankton like these krill.*

# KINDS OF BALEEN WHALES

Scientists divide all whales into two major groups, baleen and toothed. The baleen group is further split into three families—the grays, rorquals, and rights.

Altogether, there are 10 species of baleen whales and some 66 toothed species.

After the blue whale, the fin whale is the largest of the baleen group. Fins reach 80 feet in length.

The pygmy right whale is the smallest baleen whale. It grows just 20 feet long.

*The big baleen whales, along with the toothed sperm whale, are often called the "great whales" to separate them from the porpoises and dolphins.*

# GRAY WHALES

Like other baleen whales, gray whales eat plankton. They also eat small fish and animals from the bottom of their Pacific Ocean home.

Gray whales are like vacuum cleaners. They slurp up sand. Their baleen filter out the goodies. The whales must do it well for they grow to be 50 feet long.

*A gray whale reaches bottom to feed on marine animals there.*

*Scientists aren't sure why whales like this gray suddenly leap from the sea.*

Whale watchers often see grays along the Pacific Coast. Grays have crusty patches of white **barnacles** (BAR nuh kuhlz) on their skin.

# RORQUALS

The gray whale is in a group by itself. The **rorqual** (ROR kwuhl) group has six baleen whales—the blue, Bryde's (BROO dahz), fin, humpback, minke, and sei (SAY).

Rorquals have long folds of skin along their throats and chests. The folds look like pants pleats.

The folds open to turn the rorquals' mouths into huge tubs. Then the whales can gulp in tons of plankton-rich seawater.

*Rorquals, like the humpback whale, have grooved skin that stretches open when the whales feed (see page 4).*

# HUMPBACK WHALES

Humpback whales do not have humped backs. Among the long, slender rorquals, though, humpbacks do have a plumper shape.

Humpbacks make unusual undersea calls. A series of humpback notes, called a song, can last up to 30 minutes.

Humpbacks sometimes hunt by blowing rings of bubbles that settle on the ocean surface. Fish called herring feel surrounded by the "net" of bubbles.

The herring bunch together in a school. Then the whales charge into the mass of little fish and gobble them.

*A humpback whale rises from warm winter seawater in Mexico.*

# BLUE WHALES

All rorquals have a dorsal, or back, fin. They have a streamlined shape, too.

Even the blue whale is streamlined. Still, it weighs about 260,000 pounds—the same as a pile of 65 large cars or 15 bull elephants!

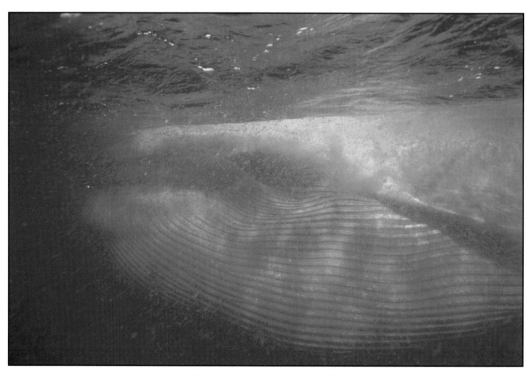

*A feeding blue whale, the largest animal on Earth, glides into a cloud of krill.*

*Like a huge locomotive, a fin whale crashes and splashes across the sea. Fins are the second largest whales. The fin's blowhole has two openings.*

The blue lives almost entirely on krill. Its baleen trap krill when the whale's tongue forces water through them.

Blue whales are protected from hunting now. They are slowly building back their numbers.

# RIGHT WHALES

Right whales do not have long flippers, as humpbacks do, but they have large heads and long baleen.

One of the right whale group, the bowhead, has baleen 13 feet long! Seen from the side, the baleen plates in the bowhead's jaws look like a great harp.

Two of the three kinds of right whales are endangered. Like most other baleen whales, they were hunted for their meat and oil.

*A right whale cruises in the sea off Argentina. Rights were named by whalers, who found them easy to catch and rich in whale oil. These whales were the "right" ones to hunt.*

# GLOSSARY

**baleen** (buh LEEN) — the tough, comblike plates found in the upper jaws of certain whales; whalebone

**barnacle** (BAR nuh kuhl) — a small, crusty clamlike animal of the sea

**endangered** (en DAYN jerd) — in danger of no longer existing; very rare

**keratin** (KER uh tin) — the tough material of which both whale baleen and human fingernails are made

**mammals** (MAM uhlz) — the group of air-breathing, warm-blooded, milk producing animals

**plankton** (PLANK ton) — tiny, floating plants and animals of the sea and other bodies of water

**rorqual** (ROR kwul) — a certain group of baleen whales with long, stretchy grooves along their mouths and chests

**species** (SPEE sheez) — within a group of closely related animals, one certain kind, such as a *humpback* whale

*A humpback's blow makes sea smoke on an early morning in Southeast Alaska.*

# INDEX